# THINGS MY HEART SAYS

## Poetry by David Solomon

?
THINKBLOT
PUBLISHING

An Original Publication of THINKBlot Publishing

THINKBlot Publishing is a division of The THINKBlot Group

Library and Archives Canada cataloguing in publication

Spence, David, 1979 –
        Things My Heart Says

                ISBN 978-0981243603

                1.      Poetry, Canadian (English)

Heart design by David Solomon
Cover Design by Matthew Ward

Published in 2013 by:

THINKBlot Publishing
Toronto Canada

Printed in the United States

For bookings and appearances | davidsolomoninfo@gmail.com | www.itsdavidsolomon.tumblr.com

To the reason why I understand what love is. I've loved you before I have ever known you. Darrius, you have made my entire life a joy as bright as your smile and as big as your personality.

I love you the morest

# Table of Contents

# Acknowledgements

Saying thank you can be hard when pride is in the way. Well I want to take this opportunity to say thank you to everyone for all their generous support in the good and bad times throughout this project. You have helped me get through and stay focused long enough to complete this book. I will forever be in debt to my brothers Edward, Jermaine, Courtney and my father you continue to inspire me, even when we didn't always see eye to eye. To those who act like family and treat me like a brother Koree (Gadget) Haye, Jason (Thought) Morris, Omari (Chef) Tomlinson, Steven (Slim) Layor, Dexter (Cookie Monster) Morris and Alicia (Thompson) Ottley you have all been there in more ways than I can count.

There are so many others who have assisted generously with words of encouragement, time, services and other efforts to make this book possible. For all the graphic work on the covers, the interior chapters and my logo Matthew Ward you are amazing. Dwayne Morgan on countless occasions I have come to you for advice and you have provided me with more help than you may know. Marina (Ree Ree) Phillips and Nathaniel Anderson for all the great conversations, they helped push and support me through this project. Kevin (Heron) Jones, you are truly great at what you do. Thank you for the long nights of editing and revisions, truly grateful.

To the team, Kujo, Blaq Roche, Trace Motivate, Ill Vibe, Lamma, Cori Green, Th3 Abyss, Silent Shadow, Ebana, GIGZ and Mindbender Supreme for all your support and understanding with not only this project, but with the music and my we show as well. I seriously cannot wait to continue working with each and every one of you.

I know saying thank you is usually taken for granted and if they are, and then that will take those for granted who deserve them. I just want to show you all how much I appreciate everything that you have done for me. Not because you had to, simply because you wanted to. Thank you from the bottom of my broken yet mended heart.

x

# Things my heart says

If you wake up tomorrow

Do more with your time

Than you did with it

Now smile!

You're Priceless

As well am I

So don't sell yourself short

Your heart's worth more

Than you give yourself credit for

The purity of love is boring

The excitement love brings

Is an adventure

It's enlightening

Change is frightening

And betrayal is disheartening

So drink up!

I love the warm feeling I get when you drink

I feel confident

When you slow me down enough to think

I feel confused

When you work off your frustration on random women

I guess that's why I'm so lonely

I know we've been through a lot

Especially since I fall in love so easily

I know it's causing you some pain

Believe me I felt every cut, slice and break

I'm working furiously to repair the damage

So there is no need for the walls I've seen going up

They're just going to make it harder for me to fall in love again

Yes I know I fall in love very easily

I've been working on this because I can't take the lonely feeling we get

Unless you drink

So I think it's time for a change

I think we should take down a few bricks a day

Erase all of the heartbreakers we've saved

Work on improving my strength

Oh, and especially your shape

Hug our lil' man more each day

He always puts a smile on your face

Remember your smile is priceless

And so am I

So let's celebrate life

While we wait for the one to cause the right kind of excitement of

adventure in our life

Now drink up!

You know I love that warm feeling I get when you drink.

# THINGS MY HEART SAYS

# Suicidal Love

Look at what you and I have become, like we refused to climb to unusually amusing heights above. Instead, we've crucified our trust and seen the view of life, DEEP INSIDE A SUICIDAL LOVE. The heart cannot process such inhuman lies and abusive crime. It hurts to survive, disgust. I feel like a nudist losing my right to decide where I can reveal my foolish kind of fun the rules of right and wrong? As if they do apply to a superman, whose music-like soothing vibe illuminates the bluest sky. I believe I'm in a race with the blinding sun, to show a flower that brings brighter proof of light. But if you don't try to inhale the fragrance, the taste of our sacred touch that fate awaits to be embracing. Then I'm ashamed that your neutrality IS TRUE SAVAGERY, more painful than blazing hatred. Hell hath no fury like a woman scorned, as if the Devil himself starts looking for an angel savior. Cause the flames of betrayal will cook your soul, like a heartless witch until you feel the opposite of positive thoughts to live long and prosper. Just toss your unwanted, sick carcass off a bridge and before you fall within the shark water's dark abyss. Take a sharp razor to carve and slit your arms and wrists. Then crash your dreams and fracture your fantasies after we stab your brain with your nose bone cartilage. I know you know hope is never hard to kill, but I'm too smart to give her all my kisses. So I'm not going to give my honor to become the martyr of modern sin, but it still feels like I've been shot and lynched. I truly thought our future unity would be obvious, but my naive confidence in your hollow thoughtlessness caused a lethal consequence. Like Romeo and Juliet and now I do regret all the lovely types of girlfriends that you didn't try to become, MY TRUTH HAS DIED. My primal lust can't resuscitate me. Woman, I hope it's you who discovers the heartbroken body of your beautiful suicidal lover.

Addi ``Mindbender`` Stewart

# Things my heart says: A Love Letter

Hey Love,

So I noticed that you said you were happy the other day, I'm glad to hear that. It's been a while since you've been able to honestly say that. I hope that this happiness continues to shine on you, I just know how hard it's been on you and a lot of times you didn't want to continue but you did. I'm really glad you did, not too sure what changed in your life but hold onto that.

I remember when you used to love being by yourself, the house was blistering with sounds from your family and you would sit quietly listening to music, writing or meditating alone in your room. You were always happy and at peace when you did that growing up, almost seemed like nothing bothered you. But for you to be so down some things must have bothered you, what was it? Was it being the middle child of 5 boys? Was it the fact that each of your brothers and even your parents shared the same month for birthday celebrations? I remember you telling me that you've had multiple forgotten birthdays' growing up. You said many times the year would end and you still weren't wished happy birthday. Years later the frequency would change and you would get a call or a text. I'm smiling right now, because that's all you wanted.

This is now. Before you were able to deal with this solitude, to avoid the pain of disappointment, did you teach yourself to treat birthdays and holidays as just another day? Was it easier than just feeling forgotten or alone? Honestly because birthdays and holidays are just regular days, but days meant to be spent with family. I know you wish that your family spent more time with you. I hope you're learning to make time special for your son.

How is Darrius by the way? I know he's getting big, is he like you in any way? 'Cause I remember you being so full of love and creativity. I always read it in your poetry and felt the love, the pain, confusion and stress amongst other feelings. You were so honest with how you felt and I love that about you. There was a poem you wrote about your father and you said you wanted to record that piece, did you? I remember you were crying when you actually wrote that poem. There was something about letting go of those feelings that really dug in deep. Your poetry always found a way to connect with those around you, but would get lost in thought when you would read them again, always second guessing yourself and how they made you feel or how good they were. Remember when Sammy came by for a drink and found one of your books on the floor? He picked it up; you said nothing and just let him go through the book. That was a big step for you; because you never let anyone read your stuff uninvited. He skipped through a few pieces and focused on one, read it a few times and said, "Man! This one right here, that's me... that's me right there".

Do you remember what piece that was? One of my favorites is "She left & my heart broke" you wrote that shortly after getting a late night phone call from one of your friends. She usually called you to distract herself from someone or work and you were always happy to be that distraction, except after that phone call. You weren't too sure if it was because you were drinking when you took the call or what, but you just had a moment of clarity and jumped right in. It was almost like you let a piece of you go, did you?

*A Love Letter*

How many times have you given up and let a piece of yourself go? I know the first time you did, you broke down and told me, you said "I never want to feel this way again so I'm going to learn how not to feel any more." And you did, you became so lifeless with people. Even when you met someone new, someone wonderful, you would still be distant. Do you think they didn't notice? Let me be clearer I know you were hurt, you wanted to marry her but didn't you think of moving on emotionally since you already did mentally? You caused the same hurt over the years that you never wanted to feel, so how does that make you feel? So I really need to know when you started feeling down again, when the happiness started to leave because I know you found it after you first were hurt. What was it that made you become so cold?

Wait, how's your family? Is everything okay with your brothers and your parents? I know you were really hurt when you starting having issues with your mother and oldest brother. Sucks too 'cause you just started to work on building your relationship back with your father. You've cried many nights for your entire family and from what you've told me it doesn't seem like things will work out or begin to change, I hope they do. How have you dealt with all of this? I hope you were able to stay focused, even though I know alcohol has always helped keep your heart warm when it was at its coldest. Have you looked into going to AA? I'm just asking, not judging. You know I love you so I just have to make sure you're good, since you have been drinking and drinking harder since you started at fourteen just to cope with all you've been going through.

Why didn't you hold fast in prayer like a lot of your poems said you did? Is it because you're an addict? I know you say that you don't have an addictive personality but come on man, just think about

xix

what you've been doing to cope and what you could have been doing. Don't you feel a little lucky to still be here? I'm really glad that you're still here, I don't know where I would be if you weren't here. It can only get better from here and I know that Darrius loves the fact that you are.

xx

I'll say this; I hope that you're happy now because you have finally started to truly love yourself. We say that love is hard and granted it is at times. I've loved; well I thought I loved and I failed simply because I did not understand the basic principle. 'Love your neighbor as yourself'. Definitely not hard to do when you love yourself problem is, most of us don't. I know there was a time when I stopped loving myself, felt that I wasn't worth being loved and maybe that's why you felt the way you did. Being your heart isn't an easy task especially when you love so hard and so easily. I hope you continue to love, because I'll always love you and that's just to start.

Love Always;


Your Heart

# My Heart

# Sins of the Father

They say I'm like you

Well, I don't see it

Blind to my own ways

So they try to reveal all the intimate details about you

Hoping that I'm a put two and two together

Never!

I've never carried a two two

Okay, so I guess that's one way that I'm like you

The only tool I've ever needed was the one I could ball into a fist when

heated

Now I know I've seen that about you

But you were quick to anger and walked away from the tough situations

I'd never walk away

Especially if that meant walking away from my little king

They say I'm just like you

Mainly when they're disappointed in things that I do

SAYING THAT I FOLLOW DREAMS JUST LIKE YOU

Know what; I am like you that way

I've been dreaming all my life

Inception! Born in it

It was a dream I had that the doctor slapped my ass at birth

In reality he was sleeping

I was in his mind and I poked him in his eye with my toe when he tried

Still I don't see how I'm just like you

We have similarities, sure enough we all do

This fruit that fell off your tree, is strange fruit

*LIKE WHEN THEY SAY, YOUR SON IS GOING TO BE JUST LIKE YOU*

I don't see it

4

Blind to my influence

I'm hoping son, that you're not like me

Your personality not rocky

Strong like a rock I mean

You have more potential and vision than my dreams have ever let me see

So I want you to dream, but not like me

I want you to wake up and grab hold of them, not like me

Work hard mentally and build your empire through education, not like me

Take your talents and your fears and combine them to create something wonderful

Don't let your fears control you and hold you back, like me

I know you're going to be a ladies' man, but don't be like me

A ladies' man with no lady, man

One way I do want you to be like me

Is by believing in yourself, the way I believe in you

That's the only way I wanna say that you're just like me

# WMM?

What makes me?

The person I am

What breaks me?

The person I am

What shakes me?

The person I am

What makes me the person I am?

I make me

My son makes me

The dreams I chase

Make me

I make me

# Favorite Colour Purple

Favorite colour purple

I changed my mind

My favorite colour red

Grilled cheese for breakfast

No I want pizza instead

Watching my shows

So Treehouse is on TV

Switch to Teletoon Retro

Transformer time for me

Outside at the park

Cars in hand

Scooting on the scooter

Oops, fell again

Dust off my hands

Before I would have cried

Toy R' Us singing "I'm a big kid now"

Ponytails and crazy hair

## NOW MY HAIR IS ALL GONE

I love my mom

I love my dad

Love my sister and my family

And my friends

But I also love to play all day

# Synonymous with you

God blessed me to give life

I cursed me with an awkward life

Frowning faces makes me feel as if the life I had

Would be better off than the life I have

The care I shared, instead of the care I share

Their care has nothing to do with me

But everything to do with me

Care is synonymous with my life

Coupled with your life

Which, is actually my life

Well, a part of my life

The life those frown on

The blessing I've been given

The curse that I gave myself is assumptive of the end result

Everyone expects me to end

End, begin within these two points

Ultimately failure is the curse I've given myself

An obstacle I've placed in my way

Your way, well my way

You were never in the way

So there is absolutely no way my curse will affect you

It affects me, by blessing me

See God blessed me to give life

I've cursed me with an awkward life

8

Time for a whole body cleanse. Free
your body, mind & spirit. So your
soul can be free. In silence you find
yourself when others find
distraction

# Fun!

What do you want to be when you grow up?

"A race car driver!"

He said with a joy that made me smile

"I'm fast, see look at my fast shoes"

"Wanna race me daddy?"

Sure, but don't cheat

Ready when you are

On your marks

Get set,

HEY!

No fair, you can't go before I say go

Giggling down the street on the way to the park

He's running for his life

He knows the tickle monster is coming out

Time to tickle the little cheater

I just gotta catch him first

Dipping and dodging

This little bugger is dying with laughter

I can't help but laugh myself

Yells from the park

"Daddy look what I can do….. isn't that cool?"

As I catch my breath

It sure is!

You're so cool too

His smile gets big

I know!

# Smile

When I see your smile

My world gets brighter

Struggles feel lighter

Hurdles leaped over

You make me work harder

Challenges conquered

Love begins to foster

In a heart that was three sizes too small

My heart beats in mourning

To the sounds of 808's and guitar strings

The wrong notes produced heart break

But when I see you smile

No more

Your smile motivates me

Bright from ear to ear

Your tiny teeth and bright eyes

Missing teeth and contagious laugh

Caring tone

With words of "I miss you too"

Your smile brightens up my tiny heart

That was cold as ice

That warms every time

I'm around you and your smile

"don't give up on anything
that you can't go a day
without thinking about!"

# IF ONLY;

If only;

We were allowed to be who we are

Make mistakes and say I'm sorry

Mean it, then move on

Even if that takes awhile, even for a lil' while

It would be nice if we could just, be

Not trying to be the rapper we see on TV

The singer whose life looks perfect, singing on stage

That Cosby household, when yours is more Adam's Family

I mean, there are so many different aspects to life

It's funny how we want everyone's to look the same

But I'm sure that when you look in the mirror you don't see my face

When you speak, do you hear the voice of someone else?

Screaming out, "HEY JENNY!"

And if I did, would everyone turn around and say

"Yeah, what's up?"

I'd hope not

That would be a lot of people named Jenny in one place

My given name is David and there is enough of us in one room at a time

To make even that, seem confusing

But I'm choosing to remain, myself

Hoping that no one is trying to be me

No one wants me to be them

That my actions would only reflect me

But they don't

Some will try and be me and others will try to change me

They will also do the same with you

But if only we could just be ourselves no matter what people think

I think life would be a lot less stressful if everyone would

Just be themselves

12

# Dreaming of D'Mies

I saw your face again as I slept last night

What a beautiful face you have

As I felt myself smiling enormously

Simply because I was looking at you

Well, not you, you, but it was you I dreamt about

Holding, playing and teaching you

To take over and be the king

Remember, you are a king

Your life path is just that big

Your footprints have already been set

They are just waiting for you to press down into them

I can't wait till your first steps

For your first fall, so I am able to pick you up and dust you off

The first time you run and jump up behind me and say "BOO"

Then we laugh and scare your mom

Since she's been so strong for so long

We can't wait for you to step into yourself

Even though I enjoy looking at you and seeing myself

Maybe that's why I'm so happy

I see so much good in you

So no matter what, be you

Every day I dream of you and pray

Excited to see my dreams of you become the reality you create

# Black Eye

Verse 1: I am the spiritual eye that shows the sinner back to God

The eye that allows the truth to be seen

The truth about being a being

In a dehumanizing situation, only built by colonization

This was meant to limit your advancement in the eyes of your peers

And those who chose to dictate hate

And I hate the fact that we cannot see

That our present is more of a struggle than the roots of our history

I continuously hear about our forefathers struggle through 400 years

Seeking reparations for the tears and tares caused by a slave master's

whip

Not realizing that our actions are causing our roots more pain

See our roots went through mounds of dirt and clay

To allow a deep history to provide its limbs with beauty

Subject to the eyes of a decolonized mind

Truthfully, your views are skewed

Fitting with today's false realities of what true blackness should be

But you can't see


Hook: you can't see

Our forefather's struggles

You can't feel

Our grandmother's pain

You just see

The bling on a chain

Your name in the game, looking for fame

So I mourn for y'all

Oh…..Oh

Let me bring you back

Verse 2: Subject to the eyes of a decolonized mind

Truthfully, your views are skewed

Fitting with today's false realities of what true blackness should be

And it's hard to see exactly what it should be

But the truth that I do see is not the images we are seeing

Nor the roles we are playing in mainstream cinema

And if it is some sort of actuality then our eyes should be red

Furious from the pain and actions caused by the black of our skin

My eyes bleed spiritually

Tears no longer pour out of me

From all the pain, violence, corruption of the madness within us

I'm saddened by the acts of our people

Everywhere we look someone's dying, no one's talking

Black people scared of snitchin'

With all the Black-on-Black violence committed daily

They don't even understand the difference between a witness and a

snitch

But you can't see

# PULSE

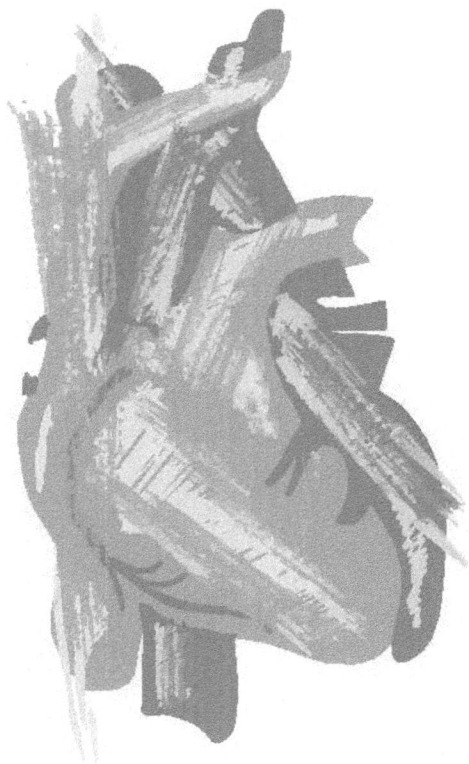

> Sometimes I wonder why I
> even bother, but then I turn
> on my phone & my sons
> smile tells me why...

# Father's Day

Thank you for being here

You could have walked away, like so many have

Leaving holes in hearts,

That hurts

They may never go away, but you chose to be a father

Who, became a dad

A man who made up in his mind

He wouldn't let his children down; you chose to be a man

And what a man you have become

The protector of your home, you are the brick house

Defending your children from the big bad wolf

Providing safety, security and so much more

Dad, you set the standards

For your daughters

You are the example they'll use for the man of their dreams

But don't be scared dad; they won't bring them if they're not legit

They watch you, so they know what a real man is suppose to be

Your sons look to you to be a father one day

They use your examples to know how to raise a child

20 But more importantly, how to treat a wife

Isn't that right fellas?

You do so much more than put food on the table

You do so much more than give us a roof to live under

Way more than put clothes on our backs

You help mould the image of today and tomorrow

What a wonderful job you've done

Thank you for being our example and filling our holes

Because of you we know what it will take to be a father

But more importantly

A man

# Seems So Natural

If I believed in past lives

Then I would understand

Why this right now feels so natural

So real

So right

So normal

Like you've been here before

Like I've been here before

Like we've been here together

Listening to the music our bodies make

Hearts pounding

The beating sound of drums

Deep breaths

Playing softly like the organ in the background

Lips kissing in patterns

The melody of our love

This seems so natural

Since I don't believe in past lives

This seems right

Like this was meant to be

The slow movements to leave

The gestures of 'should I, shouldn't I'

Then the oh why not

Follows with words we can only use

Silently

Unless the truth surfaces

22

Thinking of what we want to be

Knowing that this is too right

We might be wrong for each other

So we substitute words to ease the situation

Our attraction

Hoping that this is only a vision from our past lives

But I don't believe in past lives

So this means we have to be

That means this is just right

Even if it is the first night

No matter what it is you say
you're going to do... Just
make sure you do what you
say... - Esskei #THINKblot

# Addiction

I found myself trapped in the black hole I put myself in

I put myself in a black hole

Trying to get away from the scratching

The shaking

The cold sweats

I feel it coming up

My body is screaming

I NEED A FIX!

I NEED A FIX!

I NEED A FIX!

From the pain pumping through my veins

My blood no good

Diseased from the drugs running through my system of self-destruction

Cut off from my heart

I AM TRAPPED

24

In the black hole I put myself in

Trying to get away from the unholy thoughts I envision

The unholy actions I partake

I NEED A FIX!

I NEED A FIX!

I NEED A FIX!

Just a quick fix

A slight prick of my vein

Excitement begins rushing through my veins to my heart

A little something to hold me over

I NEED A FIX!

A quick fix from the bible

Where I hide my heart

It's hard to live the way I'm living now

Trapped in the black hole I put myself in

# Ageless Bloom

I lay in thought

Eyes closed

When I saw the timeless bloom of a flower

Pedals soft

In that moment time stood still

I've seen birth and growth

Giving life from the soil

An ageless bloom you could say

The release of her beautiful fragrance in the day

The subtle fading of her beauty as the sun sets

Her lingering presence fills the air

Overnight I bask in her beauty

In the morning

Her beautiful fragrance is exposed

At the opening of her presence

I sit and wait

To see her soft pedals

Give birth to her ageless bloom

While my eyes remain closed in contemplation

# Until it's with you

I don't want to experience life alone anymore

I want to experience my life with you

What it's like to run around with you

Play games with you

Like Trivial Pursuit just to better get to know you

Knowing what it takes to keep you happy

Until then I won't know what it's like for me to really be happy

See I've found out what it takes to be happy for a moment

I simply just have to think of you

I've found out what it takes to hold me over for a day or two without you

It's those conversations we have every night that infiltrate my dreams

But I don't know what it takes to have you

I've never got to really hold you

I've never had the opportunity to allow you to trust me

I want to allow you in, but it's hard for me

See I've been here before and I've lost

I don't know if I should

I do know, I love you without being with you

I long for you, willing to give you my all

Growing with you, is all I want

See I am done with life alone

What I want is a life with you

My life isn't worth the experience

Until it's with you

# **Drinking Xtra Stout**

My life has changed

No longer look at things based on facts

They're fake

Used to prove every and anything

Maybe that's why I'm sitting here drinking this **GUINESS EXTRA STOUT**

I hate that stuff

Maybe my taste buds changed

When I kissed that whore on the mouth

NAW!!

That's not it I walk with Listerine, so I cleaned my mouth out

Now what can I use to clean this mind up

The clutter in my mind has me running around like a lab mouse

Testing myself

Waiting for results

But the more tests I do the harder it is to make space for you

You who continuously tries to avoid me or is it me avoiding you?

You who wants me, or do I want you?

Whatever it is I need to make space in my mind for you

It's filled with questions like

Will she like me?

Why am I talking to you?

If everyone pops bottles then, who's really a baller?

If every man has more than one woman who's the real pimp?

Why doesn't every woman have more than one man?

Have you figured out what this poem means yet?

28  How do you spell my name?

What does your name mean?

Can I reach you like God wants me to?

Should I write about religion?

Should I write on salvation?

Should I speak like I'm in love?

Should I speak rationally or let my emotions take control of me?

Am I really knowledgeable?

Why am I asking myself so much questions and ignoring you?

Maybe I should stop asking so many damn questions?

Wait! Was that last line even a question?

Do you know why I think about writing for you?

Why am I Esskei?

Good question

Why am I standing here?

Don't know, can I sit beside you instead?

I should be sitting drinking a **GUINESS EXTRA STOUT** with you

NAW!! I hate that stuff

Somebody please pass me a Henny.

Do you mind?

# Tugging on Heartstrings

# S.H.E.I.L.A.

(Spring Helps Encourage Individuals Lasting Affection)

Blowing breezes from the return of spring

Uplifts my spirits

Walking briskly, through a field of resurrecting life

Feet tread over beaten paths

Sharpened on the side of the roads we last passed

The rush of excitement, forcing its way along this well lit highway

Anticipation as buzzers ring, candies popped into mouths

The sprung awaiting the arrival of spring

The beauty of the colours

The consistent cool gust of wind on an even warmer day

Feels like someone snuggling up beside you

Like the very first hug in a friendship

To the first awkward kiss starting a relationship

The sun is shinning

Transcending life from the cold of winter through spring

Right into the burning passion of summer till the longing of fall

As I think spring into existence

Coming out of my cold of winter's heart

It's time for love

32

She makes it hard for me to speak, tongue twisted, like gang sign fingers. Pointing out places, I can dine with her. Full course appetite.

## Signs of Weakness

She got me going crazy

Not off of her, sexy swang

That's too easy

She took me to places I've never been before mentally

But listen carefully this is critical

It had nothing to do with being sexual

Sure her booty made her hips rock

And I know she could have got me down to my socks

But she kept me in my pants

With talks of future plans

Dang! Ambition is sexy as hell

The sounds of success got me going and kept me steady

Pacing my way towards that checkered line

Yet no lines were drawn

She had me going all night long

Talk to me

Talk to me girl

Come on

(repeat)

We worked each other out

We tried new things

I was on the phone so long it would no longer ring

Yet I was recharged, my reception strong

I heard everything she was about, without a doubt

She presented herself well

That natural beauty got me going

But sex only, I mean it's great

But damn it

That tight warm space can't keep me coming back

I got myspace/iamesskei

And surely that can't be replaced

Just like when beauty fades

Dumb is forever they say, now dumb that can be replaced

[CHORUS]

# Wet Dreams

I open my eyes to see you standing there

"This is a wonderful way to awaken" I say to myself

A smile comes over your face

It's as if you have something in mind

Well so do I

And if you could only know what was on it

My mind is exploding with images of you

Hands running down your ebony frame

Sensual kisses on your milk chocolaty skin

Your soft & firm ass

I enjoy squeezing

Your wet, fat pussy

I enjoy licking

Your body shivers

I feel you breathing

Harder, as if trying not to moan

Ooooooooooooo

That's when my fingers begin to tickle your....

We'll call her Elmo

Elmo is laughing so hard she's crying

And tears are dripping all over your thighs

Mmmmmmmmmmm

You taste good

Maybe I should call you Campbell's

Whispering in your ear

I feel your tongue filling my ear

Pulling on my ear lobs

Making its way down my neck

My dick starts to shake

It needs a place to hold him still

Somewhere hot and firm

Some where he won't be dry

You whisper Elmo wants him

You breath deeper and harder

As I begin to fill you

Oooooooooooo

Shit my alarm went off

I'll catch you when I fall back asleep

36

"Waiting for the one not sure
if I've met her yet. So I'm not
sure what to do can't ask
everyone. Are you her? No,
have you seen her then?"

## Love Songs

Your face dances in my head

Smiling images

Every time I hear a love song

I hear your name

Wishing I was able to "JUST CALL TO SAY I LOVE YOU"

But I ain't no Stevie

And I wonder if you would even believe me if I did say it

I can hear it now, as I say

"I DON'T WANT TO BORE YOU WITH THIS, BUT I LOVE YOU, I LOVE YOU, I LOVE
YOU, MORE AND MORE"

While you reply

"ARE YOU READY FOR LOVE?"

I've had my share of "SHATTERED PICTURES"

Just in case you feel my "EMOTIONS" aren't real

37

I've cried in my pillow, dreaming of you

"IT'S ALL IN MY HEAD", "I THINK OF YOU OVER AND OVER AGAIN"

'Cause "TRUE LOVE DOESN'T LIE BUT WE WON'T KNOW UNLESS WE GIVE IT A

TRY"

Every time I hear a love song

Written about you

Written for you

In room 112

"CRAZY" amounts of times

Over you, you put me in a "SENTIMENTAL MOOD"

LIKE "NO ONE ELSE" can

I'll think of you every time I hear a love song

Hoping one day you'll say

# Dirty the clean version

Beautiful lady,

Can I spread your legs?

Ever so gently

Nibble tenderly?

Just point to where I need to bite

I promise I won't take more than I can chew

You're blushing, good

I like that reaction

Especially since I just met you

Mmmmm

I just got a thought

Let me hold you

Lay next to your sweet fine ass

Till the morning

'Cause right now I just wanna slide my

Ooops

There's kids around

So use your imagination

Then whisper in my ear what it is you were thinking

You'll be surprised to know that I was thinking the same thing

Balconies in the rain

Walls, floors, tables & chairs

I have a flair for this type of rude behavior

What's that?

Treating your body like my last bowl of ice cream

"I just hope I like it"

You will, I'm sure if you leave with me now

You'd like it and more

Like candies, flowers & shit

YES

Everyday

But not tonight

I'm trying to lose control till the sun stops hiding

So I'm a say good night to the kids as I put them to bed

And good morning to you

During your downward facing dog howling at the sun rising

Cause damnit I'm rising

So baby let's continue role playing on the balcony

40

Find me a woman I can have
a conversation with,
someone who knows who
she is & who's confident in
working on us & I'll show her
a ring

# M.i.c, h.o.u.

### (MAYBE I'M CRAZY, HARD ON U)

I love mysteries

So why don't I love mysterious women?

Don't get me wrong

They intrigue me

Well I shouldn't generalize

I mean she intrigues me

And to be honest with you

I've only just met her and she's amazing to me

I don't know what it is

Could it be the glow in her eyes

Or the crazy pics she shows

Maybe it's her honesty

I'm hoping one day she'll do yoga with me

Karma cum back here

Until she's engaged to me

God knows she's engaging

Marriage material

Maybe

Ok, I'm gassing

Pumping gas, maybe

But lord knows

She is amazing and that's funny 'cause I know nothing about her

Except she's creative and I want her

Maybe

There's just something about her

It's hard though

How can I want her when I'm with you?

# Stuck Swinging

I'm stuck on a swing

In love with two beautiful beings

Whose essence is so pure

Honestly this can't be true

It seems as if my life is worth less without them

My heart tends to sway to either side like a pendulum

Swinging back and forth between these two beauties

Torn not knowing what to do or whom to choose

I love them both

They both love me

I'd be happy if it were only that simple

Love is easy

But simply put neither beauty wants me

Even though they love me

I'm seeing perfection each time I swing to one side

Dreaming about what it's like for me with the other

This is still the least of my problems

Swinging back and forth

My problem is, they see this and don't want me

I need them to want me

Forget being friends

For one of them anyways

Again a problem I face

## Tugging On Heartstrings

Which one do I really want?

Both pure and honestly they are too good to be true

I need both, another problem

They have completed me

If I pick one then I will no longer be complete

With one I am incomplete

With both I am whole

Now I need one to compliment me

Each beauty I see

I love dearly

Love is easy

But I'm in love with two beautiful beings

Both of which don't want me

So I am swinging between the two

Until one of them do

Since I'm unsure who to pick

I have a problem and it's not love

Love is easy

My problem is I'm still stuck on this swing

# Heartache

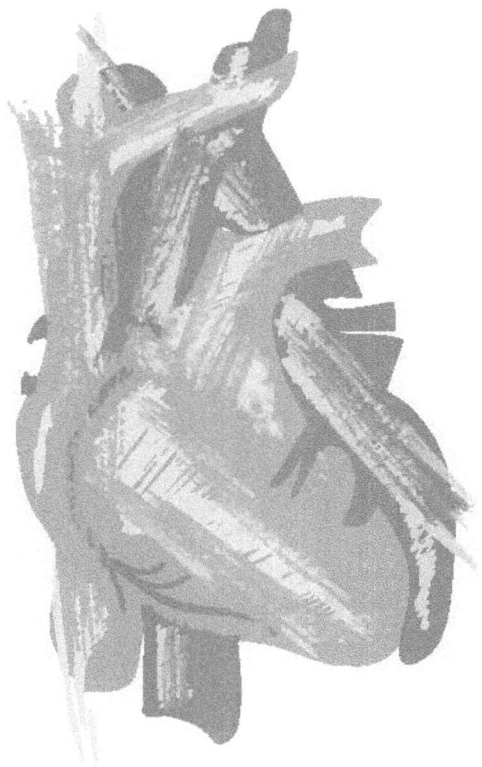

Heartache

What can I say... I like her, I
just realized though that all I
can do is like her, nothing
more. B/c she's probably in
love with him

# Things that will never be

Happiness is something I've grown to know

When I'm loneliest

I lose sight of that when I'm surrounded with hope

False hope that is

I allow myself to get sucked in to the idea of companionship

I know differently

So these are the things that will never be

Caring outside of friendship

My heart can't take the rejection

See I promised myself a long time ago that I wouldn't let myself feel this

way again

For years, every time I did I ran away

I perfected the art of building walls

Of burning bridges

Then I ran into you and poof all that was finished

Until I got slapped with the reality of the promise I made and rejected

I will never have you

I will never be happy with you here

'Cause now I'm lonely and unhappy and that isn't fair

I used to be so happy when I was alone

My thoughts were clearer

My heart was healing

Then you came along

That isn't fair because I knew together we were wrong

Still I continued to reject the promise I made to myself because of how I feel

When I know how you feel

I know your feelings aren't real

I know my feelings can't be either

I'm no longer thinking clearly, now that you're here

So it's time to go back to the promise that I made

Stay away from caring outside of friendships

They never last anyways

I think, what do you think?

48

# **Paying for Affection**

It hurts to know my feelings mean nothing to you

The simple fact is, that you feel everything is about you

Your feelings count

Your emotions matter

Your heart needs protection

While my feelings don't matter and my heart can be broken

This all seems so selfish so why go through it?

Why put myself there?

Continuing to hurt myself emotionally

Just for something I've dreamed about

Day in and day out

Since I seen your beautiful face

I've longed to be with you

But at what cost?

What price must I pay?

Before you realize that my heart is not a toy

This love thing is not a game

And eventually you'll end up lonely and bitter

If I ever get it together and leave you one day

I'm saying my heart needs protection

My feelings count

My emotions matter

But when will it matter to you?

When will you start paying attention?

# Only Me

I have a girlfriend, she has a husband

I'm not her husband, I'm just a boyfriend

Most times I'm just a friend

I am a great friend

A friend like no other

Problem is I'm not even her lover

We sneak around

Mentally

We wish we were together

I think there's a link somewhere

Only if our timing was better

Maybe if this was sometime last year

Then last year

Then last year

Let's just say it would have to be a long time ago for us to be together

But it's not

It's only me

Could I have a girlfriend that's not going anywhere?

Not unless I close my eyes and imagine she's here

I think I'll do that until she's here

Cause I'd really wish we'd be together

Her and only me

But we're not she's with her husband

And me I'm writing this letter

# Burden of the State

Mr 9-5, 7-3, 10-6, 1-9, 11-7

I'm going to 7eleven, want anything?

On my 30 minute lunch break that has me sprinting across the street

Tapping on the counter

Watching my watch

Wishing that the time would

S...L...O....W -- D....O....W......N
Damnit it didn't work

Now I'm sprinting back through the parking lot

My lunch - the baton

My co-workers in front as if running a relay race

"Keys, where are my keys?"

Damnit! They're on my desk with my fob

Now I'm late!

Here Mr 9-5, 7-3, 10-6, 11-7, 1-9

I hope I got your order right

I can't wait to get outta here

When can I get outta here?

I really don't like it here"

"Is it the hours that you work?"

Maybe we can change that and give you some joy while you're here

The only joy I can find in this is the ending of it

I LOOK FORWARD TO MY DAY, WHEN THE DAY
ENDS

The time that I'll be able to wake up & my day isn't planned by someone

who I have never met

Where my continued success is built on commitment

Not content being complacent

Not shuffled around like a deck of overly used playing cards

I work hard

At least I try to, but when you're doing things that you're forced to, it

really makes it hard to try to

It's like you're being lied to

And Mr 9-5, 7-3, 11-7, 1-9, 10-6

I'd rather be a prisoner of my own mind

Than to become a liar and content in it

Well, I would love to that is

But I've been told that I can't until I paid my rent

So until then...

Next break I'm gonna be at Wendy's

Anything you want me to get?

# Question is

What is that prize that I gotta keep my eyes on?

Another question kid

Does the prize come with a price or any add-ons?

If it does, I ain't interested

'Cause how you gonna reward me

By putting ya hands in my pocket

GET YOUR HANDS OUT MY POCKETS

Profits direct the heart to evil

My swag directs the hearts of people

Money causes men to see two's

I stay focused my roots aren't equal

Bifocals with no lenses

I spit the truth to my people

In the 40/40 with a 20/20 view

You in the 40/40 trying to catch a glimpse of J and B

Stars in your eyes is all you tryin to see

Well here's 2 shots of Belvedere and lemonade

In Cloud No. 9

I'll drink to the excitement of the paper chase

I just won't cheer when ya'll try to make it rain like Wayne and Drake

I'll mourn for the rent cheque you just blew away

Trying to live someone else's life

So my question is who you tryin to be?

# Let Love Rule?

Let's

Let

Love

Let love, rule

Well I guess if we know what love is

Believe me I would love to

I just don't think we even know what trust is

The fact that our selfishness should be an old concept of I don't want to lose myself

Eliminating the ideas of being together because it might change who I am, but being together just so we're not alone

Is this what we've come to?

Vessels consistently trying to find ourselves, constantly trying to find ourselves, constantly...

Hiding

Behind the walls we've built

Playing peek-a-boo with the hearts we've encountered

Similar to the cards we're dealt

Folding most of them with the lies that we tell

There's a self-portrait painted on the outside of your walls

As you hide you see these hearts running willingly to meet you

Surprise!

That's not you

You're not real

Let's

Let

Love

Let love, rule

Well I guess if we know what love is

Believe me I would love to

I just don't think we even know what respect is

Mostly because we don't respect ourselves

We have lost the understanding...

A smile and a hello doesn't mean they want to get it in

Simply it's incredible

How something so innocent is perceived as downright despicable

Yes I said despicable

And that's what it is

How can you be in love when you don't even respect the person within

Let's

Let

Love

Let love, rule

Well I guess if we know what love is

Believe me I would love to

I just don't think we even know what love is

56

Most people are scared to be alone, I think I'm the only one scared to be in a real relationship.. Can someone tell me why?

# Got Away

I met someone

I opened up

I let her in

I fell in love

I think its love

Now I'm not too sure

We fight a lot

I hate her guts

No I don't

I'm feeling nuts

"You are nuts" she says

I hit a wall

I pushed her out

I built a wall

I climbed over it

Then I climbed back up

To see her walking away

I want her back

I screamed "COME BACK"

She didn't come back

I met someone else

I opened up

I fell in love

I think its love

So I locked love up

The cage was open

She got away

Now I'm not so sure

She didn't come back

So I'm alone again

I hate this game

I've had enough

# **Lonely – a penis story**

We live in the realm of promise and within that realm nothing is
promised

However, everything is possible and possibly that means that things will
work out in this realm of being lonely

See I'm lonely, even though I normally don't seem to be

I am like a side mirror altering the reflection that you think you see, but
the fact is that what you see is typically not what they appear to be

My heart has no friend to call when it's down

Family is there but not always around

And after a long day of events that tends to put my heart in a vise grip

I actually can't seem to grip how I feel surrounding all of this

Basically because my mind doesn't want to have anything to do with
what my heart's been feeling

See my heart's misleading

With every woman he meets he falls in love and doesn't listen when my
brain tells him she isn't the one

So now I'm lonely and the only way that I can ignore that feeling is well,
through my penis

It's always been there for me

My male ego believes that feelings make you weak and weakness really
affects the way I sleep

Kind of reminds me of Goldie locks, or better yet Dreadie locks and too
many girls

But the locks are gone and the girls, well, they're still there playing
games

Trying to convince me that their bed is just right

Opening their doors to me so I can see just how comfortable they are

Problem is only one can be just right, so I'm caught trying to make the
right fit like Prince Charming and Cinderella.

I've found a lot that are just too soft.

They weren't able to handle the pressure after I've slept for the night I
haven't gone back; while some I snuck out in the middle of the night

One night stands end that fast

There have been plenty that have been just too hard; it took me forever
to fall asleep

So I tried them again, but after awhile they made my back so sore

They had me working like I was all of the seven dwarfs.

I don't know if it was me quitting or the bed bugs when I could rest, all I
know is that I had to go before I became Grumpy, doc

Now here comes my heart, pointing out beds that will be perfect for us

Problem is they look like the one but it never is

Something is always missing

I think something is always missing

So I sit here lonely waiting for the right Princess to come along and kiss
this frog

Until then, my penis seems to love the fact my heart and brain keep
fighting over their lists

But I'm sure my penis is getting tired of this version of lil' black riding
hood

Cause I'm seriously getting lonely in this castle alone.

# Blood Spill

*Give me drugs, alcohol &
pussy until the pain subsides
& then give it to me some
more*

# Looking Out

Verse1:

So I guess since everyone is looking out for number one

It's time for me to express my inner being

The black spiritualist, similar to a black freedom fighter

From the Black Panther Party, plus a Donnie McClurklin

We all fall down, but I'm here to give you hope

So I hope you listen to the bottom-line

I redefine facts and figures, man I hope you understand

That I'm rooted in the earth man

I'm covered in dirt, damn

You still don't get it, I'm everywhere you otta be

Similar to what you wanna be

I'm linked to the earth, so it's not hard to find me

I carry the cross on my back, the world's behind me, the bottom-line
I redefine fact from fiction, so to peep the grand scheme of things
Peep the bigger, and take a picture it will last longer
If you find yourself without a love for life you ain't going nowhere

64

Verse2:

Now I know it's hard to believe and even harder to see
That life isn't really like that, life doesn't backstab
Rubber and glue man, life is just like that
Whatever you portray, man that will come right back/to you
So mind your P's and Q's
Don't see no, hear no, speak no evil dude
And don't let evil be spoken of you
I know it's kinda hard to do when paparazzo's all up in your view
Taking pictures of all the things we knew, things that weren't true
Plus things we never knew
Who me, you'll never catch me on no cable TV
My house is made of glass so there ain't too much to see, but me!

# Stubborn

Verse 1:

Remember those days spent by candle light

And warm baths in the summer time

You'd be like Stevie Wonder, just to call and say hi

Then say I love you, now I'm thinking about the time you loved me, you

loved me not

Treated me like a bouquet of forget me not's

Man I wish it would rain, cause it's so damn hot

This heat I'm spittin' has mc's dying on the block

God it's a heat wave, long & uncomfortable

This must have made you miserable

You don't understand what this heat can do

When there's no more you

I am, Hip-Hop's Redd Foxx

If you're dead, then I'm dying slowly

I'm coming Hip-Hop!

Back to the future, like Marty McFly

This commercial ish has me all Roberta Flacked,

It's killing me softly, all you mc's are wack


Verse 2:

Now you don't understand what Hip-Hop is

You don't understand that Hip-Hop lives

Cause If Hip-hop's dead, then it's dying with me

It's dying with KRS, it died with Biggie

Its dying with Tribe Called Quest, De La Soul, Big Daddy Kane & it's

dying with Kanye

It died with Tupac Shakur, with Easy-E & again man it's dying with me

It died with Big L, flamboyant for life

It died with Aaliyah, Princess we miss you

It died with Left Eye, know TLC's nothing without you

Outkasts man, it's dying with you too

It's dying with Scarface & Jay-Z

It's dying with Guru on Primo's hot beats, man it's dying with Black

Moon

It's dying Mos, Common, Kweli, Hi-Tek, Timbaland

it's dying with Missy & Black Sheep

Mos-definitely it's dying with the Rza & Wu Tang's Immortal Technique

It's dying with LL, MC Lyte, & Nas

With Queen La, & my man Marley Marl

It's dying with Rev Run & DMC for Walk This Way

It died with JMJ, what more can I say

Abyss it's dying with you, I'm home sick so

Gigz man, it's dying with you too

# **Nervous**

I seen heaven and earth torn/the two ripped

The one in the sky small compared to where I sit

Light pierced the face of the deep/the brightness

Covered the door and the lintel/the likeness

Of the blood in an ancient land/freed the slaves

Now the ancient kings are mad

Like a racist, who ain't satisfied till we on

A slave ship, or we die in our mental state

Man face it they tempting us/reaching, grabbing

All who pass by man/they pulling them in

With sweet pleasing objects and spinning rims

That still has their heads spinning/I'll tell you this

Bling compared to the bling of a king is dull

Shapes and figures are easily lost with age

Twenty-one is the max for most inner city youth to look to the sky for

grace

But I

I saw the son crying/nailed to the old rugged

Crucifix, man I sure did

And Christ came to fix it/well so have I

Following my predecessors/Soul I'll rise

Instead of being pulled down through the cracks of society

Man, life has already been cut down
And all our natural resources are fading away
You hear the sounds of timber deep in the rain forest
Shouting 5-0 and bubba yelling "RUN FOREST RUN!"
Through the concrete jungles/RUN!
Cops shout assume the position, echo's the judges gavel
He passes his sentence of rehabilitation
Twenty-three hours a day
Welcome to the bottomless pit, otherwise known as hell
Says Jah Cure, from behind these prison walls
Looking for restoration while he sits in his cell
But I

The streets bleed, corporations take/they're full of greed
Based on the things that I've seen
Let me plant a seed in your seeds/to form some understanding
'Cause right now the truth is not landing
It's hitting deaf ears, the black box is not here
Now that's what I call a hell date
If you don't listen this will be your fate
You'll be down at the bottom/this is ground zero
Fighting for nothing, they're fighting for cash
Your life's in debt, now they're forcing your hands
To make some changes, they're drastic, they're dangerous
A teller's dead/your daughter's aunt is in the dumpster
The plan counter fired and I'm not envious
Green the only colour that matters in this life you live
Fighting for dead presidents
The death never ends till I look up and I see the two rip

68

# You

Verse 1:

Time to face the mirror and deal wit you

Twisted foundations, builds for a strong ground work

You can't look and see your head's in the dirt

You don't understand respect like putting in work

You think money comes fast, so you press the gas

You need to enroll in my school for scoundrels

I mean H.I.S. school for the unknown, like Common Sense and realize

that you use to love her now that Hip-Hop's dead

All the hype has gone straight to your head

Pen and pads, fine tuned guitar strings, all that music's dead

You'd rather hear Rich Boy than my man Louwop

Rip it or bounce to Swizz Beatz than hear the, unknown producer

GIGZ you're crazy, the grimiest, I'll call you sicko

Man you hear this, you need to know

Hevhanli ill Soul is here for the creation of the still sick soul

Till the death I rep the still sick soul


Hook:

You can't even speak on this

You can't even see your mess

You can't even hear this tune

'Cause your soul is so far gone

You're the sick soul, man you lost control

Bridge:

So why I gotta live the little miss sunshine life

Call D.R. Phil to patch things up nice

Betta yet sideshow like Jerry Springer

I'd rather be like Marge and Homer

Who needs the Kwiki Mart, right

But to get some J-E-LL-O Pudding Pops

Can I be like Cliff and Claire tonight?

Verse 2:

Please compare me to the great Lou Rawls

When you hear Esskei, man you've heard it all

The stories never ending so I'll end it

You just occupy the pages within it

Loose translation, man we're finished!

You are no good to me

Like pork is unclean

You insight the rage in my soul

I'm a savage beast

I flee the scene

Back to the mirror, back to you

I still have a lot of things to deal with you

So please give me a tissue so I can wipe away your tears

A man's gotta cry sometimes but have no fear

When you're living this life, it's a long road to travel

Put you on a 45", It's a rocky road

## Blood Spill

The road is so rough

My name is Esskei and the road's not that tough

Man it's like a pimp, call it Fillmore Slim

But instead of bowin' down, fold five and swing away like Frank Thomas

I'm in the major leagues, I play for major teams

Liberate your mind, body and soul so your soul is free


Hook:

You can't even speak on this

You can't even see your mess

You can't even hear this tune

'Cause your soul is so far gone

You're the sick soul, man you lost control

71

# Alone

Hook:

I'm all alone, sitting in the spotlight is anybody even here (x2)


Verse 1:

The spot lights, really the street lamps

Winter has come, it's cold

Winds blowin' through my parka, I'm cramped

Can't take it

Nowhere to laugh

My mind – is filled with pain

I used to be warm in the heart, when the liquor came

Times have changed

Walked away

Now I'm here again

I've never felt the same

I try to be all that I can, at times it's so hard/I can't even father

myself/tried to work it out

It's hard to be you when your back's against the wall and there's no way

out


Verse 2:

It's one thing to be who you aren't

It's another to be accepted for the person you are

*Blood Spill*

The choices you make, the decisions you take

The pathway you decide to face

All the friendships that once were, sometimes never make it

Can you find a way out, I don't know if I can

I'm only here for a moment of time

Trying to find out why I'm alone/sitting in this cold, cold world/I tried,

I've tried fighting, but I can't

# Round and Round

**Verse 1:**

Your wandering eye has me wondering

If you love me for me

It's crazy I feel like I'm chasing your love

And you knew I was losing it

> **Bridge:**
>
> See but I'm scared of this hatred
>
> That I'm feeling in my veins
>
> Said I'm scared of this love
>
> That I've been chasing

> **Hook:**
>
> Round and Round
>
> And Round (x3)
>
> Yea, Yea

**Verse 2:**

I know that you don't love me anymore

See I know that you don't care

See I know that you've been creeping on me

Now when I see you, see I don't care

> **Vamp:**
>
> I'm tired of this empty love (x4)

**Outro:**

I know that you've been creeping on me

And I know that you don't care

# Great Emcees

(V1): Raise a fist with me for the great emcees/The ones who fought violence by non violent means/The ones who stood for peace, who stood up in the streets/Got cuffed by the jakes, for taking a white man's seat/Seriously! Keep our heads up in the face of danger and in hatred through history I hope to God y'all want more/It's time to lead, we ain't lame is we/And if we is, take notes from the King of all Kings/Rise up and walk/In '63 & '95/One million rose. One million more marched in line/to the beat of a drum/the ratta tat tat of a peaceful one/Sounds stronger than the music blasting outta your trunk!/You should have heard the hums!/Of the Civil Rights Movement, moving through your tweeters/But instead you heard the nooses, tightenin' around your neck like gooses/(It's time to protect that neck son) = adlib

*Bridge:*
Huey P., Martin Luther King, Malcolm X
Gandhi, Marcus Garvey, Chavez
This is a list of the great emcees

*Hook:*
Raise a fist for the great emcees * 2
Come on get your hands up
Raise a fist for the great emcees * 2
Come on get your hands up

76

(V2): Raise a fist with me for the great emcees/The ones who stood up for peace, but fought by any means/The ones who wore the bow ties, leather jackets and the berets/Fought strong in their community/Against the haters, KKK, the naysayers and the sell-outs/The ones who sold you out for 30 pieces of silva/man, get the hell out/This is history, do you know what you did to me in '65, 2nd month, 21st day/Ratta tat tat/It's the sounds of a gat/People's are screamin'/Brother Malcolm just went down like that/The nations cryin'/1 year later Panthers burst into town/Huey P. and Bobby Seale straight looking around, for more/2 years later it's the sounds of war/ Ratta tat tat /the sound of another gat/They shot Brother Martin down on the balcony/I hear the world cry out/(MAN WHERE OUR LEADERS AT!) = adlib

(V3): Raise a fist with me, for the great emcee/The one who stands for non-violence & peace by any means/The one whose spirit fights against the murderous machine/Against the ignorant, backstabbing so called spirited regime/With peace, love & respect./Bless, yes it's me/I'm the emcee, the next voice you'll hear/I'm revolutionary/Speaking knowledge that got your mind open/Man/Don't front, you know I got you open/Got you open & you're hopin', that it wouldn't get to this/But in 1881 we know that slavery ended/So why in the world are we still fightin'/Jena 6, white tree, negros still frightened/Still hidden away, from change/So called educated/we still whipped, so barring these chains/Black men fill prisons not schools, they fill graves leaving babies after 50 yrs/(What the hell have we changed) = adlib/Nothing

Gandhi, Martin Luther King, Malcolm X, Mother Teresa, Huey P. Newton, Yogananda, Bobby Seale, Buddha, Rosa Parks, Che, Nelson Mandela, Chief Apostle Monroe Saunders Sr., Jesus Christ

# I need you

(OPEN UR EYES)

Hook:

I need you

To open up your eyes

(Chords: cmaj7, am, em, g6)


V1:

I know where you're going / and where you need to be

Sometimes you're hoping / other times it is greed

The stories from the ghetto / Can't escape the movie screen

Struggles and the heartache / Roots can always be seen


V2:

Slave to my existence / I need a clearer way

The cotton fields are empty

Yet I still hear the slaves / singing songs of freedom

Waiting while they wade / in polluted distant water

Trying to find their place / sayin'

# Today's Name is Tragedy

**Whispers**

"Why'd you do that?" "What you doing?" "Don't tell anybody" "Don't say that(...say that..say that) echo " "What"

**Intro adlib**

They say, when you lose someone. You pour liquor. Well Fuck it, here's the bottle

**Poem**

I'm so hurt, my heart's torn (breathing)

Rent itself into pieces

The pain of losing you I must mourn, (momma why'd you go) the hurt you felt

The uncertainty of not knowing (momma *echoing*) is so much more than I can feel (momma)

My heart hurts from the pain I feel (I need you), knowing I'll never see you again (momma where'd you go)

I wanna be selfish

And have you all to myself (why'd you *echoing* where'd you go)

OH GOD

Why did it have to end this way?

Such a hard life to end in a tragic death (moaning NO)

A prolonged unknowing, with a look of no hope

Feelings of pain (I can't make it)

Here we go again (I can't make it)

I can't think (you'll make it)

Today's name is Tragedy

Today is a day I want no part of (I'm outta here)

My heart has rent itself into a million pieces (I'm sorry)

(let me go) I hope to lose the piece called today

I can't speak (breathing)

Can't breathe

Can't see my eyes are closed (choking breath)

This must be a dream (what's going on?)

AM I FUCKING DREAMING (where am I?)

(this can't be real) Whispers of hope, like white noise static (what's

happening?)

Hitting my damaged ear (breathing HELLO *echoing*)

(where you at?) You can make it, I don't need saving I'm hurt

(too late moan) I can't think with all this noise (who said that?)

My chest sounds like major construction rendering itself to pieces (why's

it so loud?)

Grinding my heart into dust (what did you say?)

I can't lose today

Brushing the dust away from my feet (get off me)

Looking for a glimpse of you, of me (why's it so loud in here)

The smile I had before this tragic dream (hello)

But I can't find it

I've searched (let me out)

Hunted

Panicked

But it's not here (where am I?)

I'm not here (choking breathing)

You're not here (momma *echoing*)

# **Dear Hip-Hop**

**(V1):** Dear Hip-Hop I know you're alive/but I'm paying my respects cause a part of you died/you're a body, they took your old voice away/still a baby, so I'm guessing that it's time to change/The beginning of your birth, Grand/Came like a Flash/The message was sent and Kurtis Blow, Blew right past 'em/Paving the way for LL to Rock the Bells/MC Lyte grabbed the mic and Slick Rick had a story to tell/Rest in Peace to DJ Scott LaRock/While KRS-One broke down the word Offica/Man that was hot/Public Enemy told us what to fight for/Later Arrested for Development of our minds and flows/From Special Ed to Biz Markie/While the Chubbsta disappeared to get a degree/We had Maestro Fresh conducting things and lady Michee Mee spittin that real Jamaican funk.

**(H):** Hip-Hop/ Is more than Rap music

Hip-Hop/ is b-boys and dj's

Hip-Hop/ is graff writing and b-girls

Hip-Hop/ is self expression started out for the youth to grow

Hip-Hop/ it's more than just art

Hip-Hop/ it speaks from the heart

Hip-Hop/ it was never a treat

Rap music caught on fire now we're standing by its grave

**(V2):** Wash your face in my sink like the Warriors/who Dream a lot, catch the intricate plot/We rise like the sun sometimes and then we fall/into cash crops from figure IV leg locks/Like the Lox/Bad Boys in

shiny suits/We had a lot of Ghetto Concepts/But not Too Black
Guys/Master T and Da Mix/It's Mathematiks the way we break down
our concepts/Conceptionalized into Kos/So tell me what does it take to
make it/Heaven only knows/So we put a Northern Touch on it/Picked it
up from the roots/Here's the foundation of Hip-Hop/Chillin in my b-boy
stance/From Baby Blue Sound Crew to Starting from Scratch/Take it
back before Bakardi Slang/One for the money/Yes two for the
show/Pause

**(H):** Hip-Hop/ Is more than Rap music

Hip-Hop/ is b-boys and dj's

Hip-Hop/ is graff writing and b-girls

Hip-Hop/ is self expression started out for the youth to grow

Hip-Hop/ it's more than just art

Hip-Hop/ it speaks from the heart

Hip-Hop/ it was never a treat

Rap music caught on fire now we're standing by its grave

**(V3):** Okay here we go again and the trend says/That we have to lean
and rock and even have to two step/I know it's offensive most women
can't take it/Sliding credit cards down them while they're naked/Even
though it's offensive, the radio plays this/Someone out there said the
radio needs this/I know man that the radio needs this/Yo GIGZ please
tell them that "The radio needs this"/And I hope and pray to God that
the radio plays this/Cause Kanye got a hit when he walked with
Jesus/Man I walk with Jesus and I rap with God/Screaming out, OH
MY GOD!/Yellin' Raw Raw Raw like a dungeon dragon/There you go
again man with your pants saggin'/So how you going to dance to
this?/Pick up your pants, jump around and Rock ya hips.

# Hell and Back

Why would I feel for a world that feels not for itself
Now I'm dead to this world and my shit, man I'm going through hell
Why would I feel for a world that feels not for itself
I swear, I'm dead

Man I'm going through hell here
My mind is so clouded
It feels like I'm free falling through all of my fears
Steady catching the dreams, I help steal 'em
Now I'm hitting the snooze button on all my tears
Yea! And momma said, momma cried
But I never thought the day would come when I would leave her side
But I'm here, standing all alone with my seed
Despite the fact that niggas thought I wouldn't be
Strong enough to make it in this game
So I'm pouring out some liquor for you lames
It's a got damn shame
That the world is going up in flames
And I swear that the only thing that I can say, is

Why would I feel for a world that feels not for itself?
Now I'm dead to this world and my shit, man I'm going through hell
Why would I feel for a world that feels not for itself?

I swear, I'm dead

I'm going through hell and back, my heart is so cold
It started with the lack of love and the lies that you've told
Put my pistol to my lobe, come on pull the trigger
I'm working hard to separate myself from these niggas
Had to separate my heart from the one I love
I lost her once so I'm looking to the sky above
To regain my soul, I cut off my locks
Cause everybody's trying to put my ass in a box

Laying in my bed, hoping today is tomorrow instead
Wishing that when I wake up, I don't pray I was back in yesterday
'Cause today is filled with so much pain and tomorrow ain't promised no way
So when the world's going up in flames, all I gotta say

Why would I feel for a world that feels not for itself?
Now I'm dead to this world and my shit, man I'm going through hell

# Blood Spill

Heartache, love's fake.

All it takes is one break.

To change ya mind state from floating on cloud 9.

To falling then your heart breaks.

You did some hard time.

Now look the condom broke, life's full of mistakes.

Wrong time, wrong place;

You need that bail money fast, no games.

The outcome wasn't funny.

To release you from this hell you smoke, till you're as high as when you fell.

Never thought I'd make it here

Walked through the footprints to my soul

And I told her to take care.

I told her to go home

I can't fear being alone anymore.

Just look at how far I made it on my own.

They say, there's one footprint in the sand, 'cause God is carrying you in his hands.

Well, I feel as if I was told to walk the same path, until I felt the warm water touching my soles in the sand.

I never felt the warmth

The only thing I ever felt was the cold in the town where I'm from.

Where I live, the hate will consume you if you're smart you'll use it as
fuel too.

Drive by the haters, waive to all the haters

I'm going in, with 2 cups of Styrofoam.

And some fuckin' dark rum in a packed room.

Not feeling so young.

Eyes covered by dark shades, no sun.

It's too soon to hide my tears caused by my open wounds, scarred with
my fear.

Two shots to mask my pain.

Two more over here

Black is what I'm tryin' to see.

If I see tomorrow then tomorrow's what I see.

I can't remember today.

Depression fills my brain, with thoughts of all the haters in every single
city that I claim.

Make sure my premiums are up-to-date.

Then go out on this date, with this bad bitch that I hate.

Hard liquor is coursing through my veins.

Living in a world that I hate, using a word that I hate.

I see six feet of dirt piled by my grave.

God I hope it starts to rain.

So I can try and drown in my tears before the weight takes my pain.

While I watch loved ones throw dirt on me telling me they care.

I really couldn't care, I'll just watch and fade away.

I'm over all the hype, love won't change a thing.

I'm done!

Open up the gates

# Broken

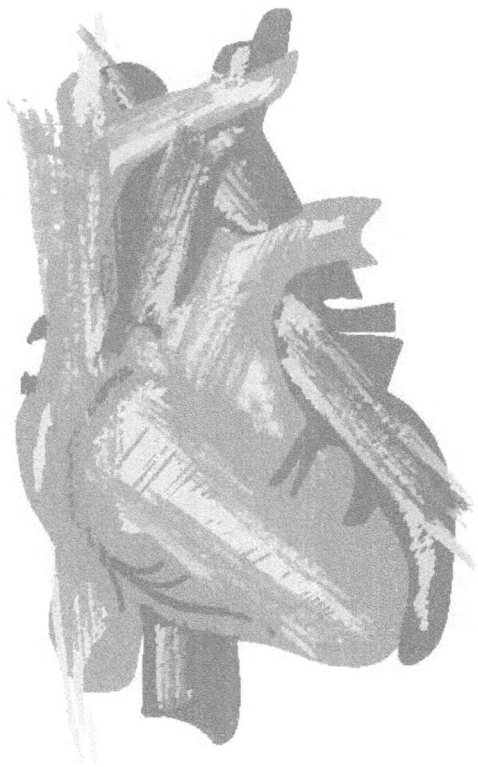

# Different Especially

You loved me especially
Different especially *2
When I'm with you
You loved me especially
Different especially *2
I still love you


This used to be so natural
My heart pounding with excitement
When I enter into your presence
My heart skips a beat - Now I'm off beat
I'm trying to catch my timing
I gotta find a way to put the time in
I'm cooking so I'd put the thyme in - And I'd be lying
If I said I wasn't in love from the first time we locked lips and hips
And tried to fight this feeling - what was happening
It felt so right
Now look what's happening
I'm leaving and I'mma say good night - This isn't right
It's not something that I'm used to
I was getting used to - Being off beat
Feeling my heart skip, skip - skip a beat
It felt so natural when I was with you

Now I miss you

Wish you – would still say

You loved me

'Cause I love you

You loved me especially

Different especially *2

When I'm with you

You loved me especially

Different especially *2

I still love you


You don't say it or act it

Or give me the chance to feel – The way we used to

My stomach is in knots

From the thought of losing you

eharmony

isn't going to catch a profile of me – to search for you

I've searched for you

From the moment I could breathe

I meditate that I'm holding you

Trying not to breathe – breathe

Breathe

If that means you leaving me – baby please don't leave

Its hard enough to believe – that I left you for my ego

Cause we go

Way back like Mario & NES – baby I'm a mess

I'm just lost without you

*Broken*

I need to change!

If I gotta kill my ego just to get back in

Bridge the gap again

So I can hear you say

"You can stan' still"

From this moment I'm a stand still

'Cause I'll always love you

You (echoed)

Till I stand still with you


Whether near or far

You used to love me

But not no more

More or less I'm in this alone

Alone to love

Love you continuously

Endlessly

Eternally reflecting my love for you

You loved me especially different

Even when my ego loved me more

I loved you

> Depression & a 3some. Who
> else feels depressed but still
> sleepin around?

# She Left & My Heart Broke

### (red dress)

For years I smiled when I heard your voice

My heart went "buduff"

Right before, during and after being near you

I've always been there

Always been your friend

Admitted how I feel

Well, felt

Expressed my commitment to making us work

Played the gentleman and never tried to push it

Never felt I had to, 'cause I knew we both felt it

You just didn't want anything to do with it

I was simply a distraction

*Broken*

An attractive friend that was a no, no until your relationships ended

For years I was your spare

Wishing that you would get a flat

Just so I would feel needed

Well, it never happened

And now I'm rusting in the trunk you left me in

The car you had when I was there

You just happened to give it away

You gave me away

Left me broken hearted

My heart hurts

My smile isn't the same

When I realized that I would only be a friend designed to relieve you

I'm perfect if you need a break

You broke it when you walked away

Now my heart doesn't "buduff" any more

# Horoscope Assumptions

Some people swear I'm apathetic

Emotionless and miserable

Unenthusiastic and conditional

They feel I'm confrontational

Educated, yet ignorant to how they feel

They call me an asshole

Selfish and needy

This sounds like a horoscope description to me gee

Actually all that's missing is something to look out for or look forward to
today

Well, maybe I'll add that now

Let's say;

Today, you'll encounter a misunderstood soul

Someone whose feelings are extra sensitive and hand you'll need to
hold

An individual, you barely know

But swears they know you

And for the love of heaven

Swears you know them too

So watch out for the confused, yet warm hearted

Any long encounter will cause you to leave them broken hearted

Okay now that makes me feel a little better

But now I'm hearing moans from the broken hearts from underneath their sweaters

They say that I'm proud and need to give it up

I need to learn to love and find a way to trust

That if I continue I'll be alone and lonely for ever

Miserable and moody regardless of the weather

I guess,

Maybe it's time for me to bring my umbrella

'Cause all I'm feeling is tears from some self-appointed judges

Ya'll need hugs?

I'll be sure to give em

'Cause all I'm a do is just smile, grin and bear it

The truth I cherish

The truth is ya'll don't know me and it's apparent

The ideas you have of me

That's been created in a world of illusions and self-hatred

They may not be exactly as you think they are

I'm just sayin'

Kind of like the passenger side mirror

Your judgment is off, and you're not checking your other blind spots

Weird

So how do you expect to get a better view on our positions?

CRASH!

Now we're both damaged and you have no insurance

You assumptive ass

Silence, I hear it, I hear it

All because you wouldn't listen

# I Haven't Found

Why do I look for such messed up dreams?

Knowing, they won't all come true.

No I'm not mad, but I do know

Your conscious is your unconscious

And your unconscious your subconscious

Known as the reality in which you live

Now is your future

Your future your present

And your past is where you is

Take my place and picture yourself up here

Your mind thinking of what to say

While your mouth says things other than what's on your mind

To use words and fill the void on the blank piece of paper in front of me

That doesn't even exist

Now is the time where grammar and politically correct aren't always right

Because I took what you said, flipped it and made it mine

Does it make it right?

Does it make me wrong if I decide to use nigger in a song?

I'll be the "Last Poets'" mascot

In fact I hear cheers for more

Saying

"Esskei, Esskei"

My subconscious is running away to get on stage

*Broken*

My conscious already reciting Sly Stone

Don't call me Nigger, whitey

Don't call me Whitey, nigger

Oh how I wish my unconscious stopped me

I feel wrong, my egos gone

I'm no longer writing on pages that do not exist

It's right here

Thousands of loose leaf sheets

Reaching out for me

Every page blank but one

In the realm of reality I know I've helped someone reach that place

As I leave the stage

My mind dissipates, and my future blends with the past of the page

My pasts have been erased

The stage empty

In the existence of reality

I see my cold fate

# Pin BLOCK

Unanswered text messages

Pin requests denied

Difficult conversations

Broken hearts

Teary eyes

Lost words

Misplaced rhymes

Limit my comprehension

Broken hearts

Teary eyes

Bonds built broken

Lifelong friend's foes

Wishing we can communicate

Praying the wounds would close

Unanswered text messages

Pin requests denied

I think I lost my best friend

Broke hearts

Teary eyes

If you knew what I know &
have been through what I
have you'd be in a padded
room. I just gotta thank the
heavens for this blessing of
not going crazy

## Stressful

Without the stress, that's how I wanna live

That's how I wish each day would begin

As free as the air that I breathe when I sigh in pain

As I exhale

When I think about the very next breath and all the stress it's gonna

bring

I inhale

I wanna throw my hands up and SCREAM

Then quickly kick the chair away before I exhale and my mind is

changed

Too late

Now my mind's insane

Taken over by everything that scares me shitless

I'm gifted

The gifted is sitting in the corner, curled up as an infant, in an infant's pose

And in an instant rocking back and forth

Screaming silently for no one

Fighting within himself 'cause he's lonesome

How come

When there are so many people around him

He's scared of the outcome

How come

Because no one knows him or supports his goals as they are

They just try to change them

And attack his hopes

Maybe this is why he feels so alone

And needs a doctor's note

A padded room and a night nurse

Before it's too late

His spirit is broken from the stress to please them all

# Hopeless

I feel hopeless, like a penny with a hole in it

And my heart seems to be attracted to the pain of it all

Squeezing through my hopelessness

Feelings of it all, only leaves my heart bruised from the stress of

attempting to fit in with the rest of those who are as hopeless as I am

Who don't know that the penny has a hole in it

So to them, they're fine with the stresses that they face

Temporary moments of ignorance

Has them pursuing dreams the penny is suppose to help fulfill

Flicked and flipped from between my finger tips into the pool of tears

from all who dreamed before me

I prefer a pill to sedate my faith

Opposed to looking through these pennies trying to pinpoint where my

hope caved

Searching for another penny as I walk past my grave

All I can seem to find is pennies without a face

I guess I should face it

You need more than a penny to change this hopelessness

# **Someone Else**

I'm in love with someone and the feeling's so wrong

I think I'm in love, because these feelings are so strong

I wanna be in love, because I've hated the feeling for so long

But I really just don't think I am the feeling feels just so wrong

Like seriously, I just met this person

How can I possibly feel this way?

Plus they already love someone

And I already told Sienna that I'm the main dish

I'm not a side plate

Like, look at me

Do I look like carrots, potatoes and broccoli sautéed in garlic butter with a pinch of sage?

No, no I don't

But it sure does sound good

Wait, that's not the point

See this is what I do, I get confused

Food my substitution for love

So to tie the two together I cooked for her

Poured a glass of wine

Hoping to alter her plans

From thinking about someone else

While locking eyes over dinner plates

Where's that ice cream?

It didn't work

# Love's Too Much

I never thought there'd come a time, that you wouldn't be in my life

Your love's just too much to hold

It's amazing, seemed so natural

For many years, history compared

It was magical under the mistletoe

But that was then and this is now

'Cause I loved you, just count to ten


I love you, but your love's too much for me

Love's too much for me (repeat)

I love you, but your love's too much for me

Just too much for me

Love's too much for me, just too much for me


Where do we take our love from here

'Cause what was commitment now feels like a chore

The seasons changed this is clear

What was eternity, now is no more

Too much deceit, too much pain

Too many lies from you to stay in this thing

Can I let you go?

I gotta let you go, 'cause love don't live here no more

# Closure

# I Trusted You

You loved me

I loved you

You broke my trust

When you walked away

Said you'd always be there

I trusted you and love conquered

I rebelled against love

Felt love was the cause of your lie

No matter how hard I tried

Love always found its way into my heart

So I lied to myself, said love wasn't there

To those trying to get in

Lying to you, even though love was there

It was my trust that was grim

Paranoid emotions wouldn't let me trust that quick

I had to protect me

108 Against all the foreshadowed heartbreaks I'd face

I refused to learn how to trust again

That made my lonely heart ache

See it was your distrust that started my fate

As I promised myself that if I ever gave my heart away after this

If it was ever stepped on or misused

I'd never give it away again

So I didn't

Pretended I did and broke hearts on the way

Caused the same pain I didn't want to face

I'm so sorry for that to everyone I faced

For putting you through the same pain that I hate

It broke me

I just hope I didn't break you

With the love that I role played

Yes part of it was fake

It was all because of the trust I couldn't take

# The Midst of Darkness

The sky is so clear

Looking down on the lights

Beyond the horizon

Shimmering patterns

Glow in spots of darkness

As if to say

You are never alone

High in the sky

Looking down as if I am looking down from heaven

I see in the midst of darkness

Hope in knowing I am not alone

# Silence

Listen to the sound of silence

It's simplicity

The stillness of fear

Nothing

The calming feeling of emptiness

Being in awe of creativity when silence creeps in

I've been basking in silence ever since you've left

I've been taking in nothingness

As I've sat still focused on me

I've sensed an overwhelming calm

At first I felt empty in the moments of silence

The stillness was a reminder you had gone

I sat in awe of silence healing

When I've been creative

Looking at what I've created while being in awe of silence

I'm silent

I've grown, in silence

In silence I feel complete

In silence I've accepted truth

Now in silence I'll wait for you

Love is simple, but we
complicate it.. Why bc we
don't love ourselves enough
to simplify it.. "Love your
neighbor as yourself" - simple
no?

# **Wrong I**

Turning in my seat towards the window, all I could see was trees and
lights in my right eye
My wrong eye allowed me to see the shadow of the man of God
Who I left as I turned
I began weeping after being told I was going to hell for holding a grudge
I AM NOT GOING TO HELL OVER ANY MAN!
But I just can't seem to let go
My right eye catches "dad 3" in graffiti on the side of my hurt
In fact there are many things tagged on my hurt out of anger
Rebellion

I feel the pain of male pride taking away my childhood innocence

My wrong eye only saw a shadow of the man of God

Huh, the shadow of the man of God telling me to trust

Telling me to love

Telling me to let someone love me

I DON'T KNOW HOW!

I never knew how to trust a man

I can't even trust myself

But I'm suppose to forgive "dad 3" so dad can forgive me

So that I can be a daddy who is seen by the right eyes

As the tears fell

My wrong eye caught a glimpse of the light shinning from the man of
God

Saying "the only thing you can do is try"

I cried

All night

Thinking about "dad 3" and the dad I was going to be

And I wanted to be free

Breathe

# Monumental

Verse 1: I'm letting go of all the pain, the hurt, the anger

All the tears I've cried, for years I've lied

On my face asking my savior why, you were the man you are?

And why must I Live life linked to you

Call you father and have respect for you

You never protected me, respected your wife or your seed

But still you expect me to believe that you love me

Love me how?

When you weren't even present for my birth man

You missed my first, firsts

First breath, first steps, first words

When I tried calling for you, you never heard me

Yelling for my daddy, father, donor/look what you became to me

Man it's plain to see, that how I feel is a reflection of how you really

treated me

So I wonder inside myself, if I could do anything to help this life

That I'm living, 'cause you know it hurts me right

From all the days of crying late at night

Wondering why my father didn't try, to make all my dark days bright

Wondering, why aren't you here with me now

It's okay, the Lord is here with me now


Hook: Why are you here with me now/

I know that you`re here with me now

Lord I need you now

The pain in my heart hurts so bad

And the stress is just weighing me down

114

Why did I let you leave

I didn`t mean to make you leave

Stand next to me

Stay in my heart and protect me at the same time connect with me


Verse 2: You left, why did you leave?

No word, no warning/I couldn't believe

After we sat down/hashed out

Tried to work out our problems

You dissolved hope by walking out

Moms calling you worthless/man you worthless

And over time you started to prove this

By screwing your kids

How could you screw your kids,

After you said you loved us/look what you did

You followed the trend where love is I, I, I

While I try to hold back this anger and try, try, try

To love you again, yes you

I love you I said

And even though I dread

That I'll be just like you

With my thoughts locked in my head man here's what I said

# 1month 2soon

Love me more today than you did yesterday

Tell me you'll never leave me no matter what

You'll be there for every touch

Experience me as a new challenge

One that gives you joy to face and conquer

To share with

To shelter

To protect and defend

Love me like you've loved no one else

Make our experience the greatest you've ever had

Limit nothing when it comes to us

Gain everything for the sake of us

Force nothing let everything be beautiful in its own space

Do all this for me

And I promise you will only get the same from me

It's my sunflower promise

# #iWin

*clearing throat*

It came to me as clear as a day in August

I'm bigger than you think I am

Bigger than you would ever allow me to be

1,000 times stronger than you feel I am

Hell, I'm talented and you make me believe as if I ain't got no skills

Well, no more

I'm calling for change

I see a reflection of Obama

The fighter hiding deep inside reminds me of Mohammed in his prime

See sometimes I lose focus and I let your negativity creep back in

Like a winter draft

Your cold heart hits me deep in my bones

Well, no more

I have a bag of dreams

One is to be free from your tyranny the way King dreamt it would be

Another, is to affect my community with the heart the Panthers gave

But that kind of change hurts my heart knowing I'mma ride alone

So I locked it away

I'm protective and I need to protect myself from you

I'm sitting under a tree you say is restricted to you

Still I sit there anyway knowing what your kind will do

Well, no more

*Closure*

I ain't standing for this

My foundation; the stone chips my brother Malcolm busted up and

dusted off

When he landed on Plymouth rock

So by any means, I'm goin' in

Hard on anyone who tries to limit who I am

You don't know me

My possibilities are endless and lames like you don't get it

Well, no more

I'm a win call me Usain

I found my lane and I'm a stay in it till the tape pops

Make sure that I'm the first one to make the tape pop

I'm old school

But new enough to delete you punk

I don't need you or anyone who don't believe what I got

iWin!

*Wipes the spit off the bathroom mirror*

# May 22

When you left I sat in silence

Holding my phone

Wishing every time that red light flashed I would see your name

I'm waiting on my phone to ring

But I know that won't happen

You have a love and he isn't me

I knew what this was before you even came

Still I was hoping that your love would change

"She left & my heart broke"

My BBM status I rearranged

In hopes that you saw my pain

And I know it was selfish of me

But my heart doesn't feel, that this right here is fair

See today started and I was full of excitement

My heart was overwhelmed

I didn't know what to do

Since the last time I felt this way was

Umm well

So long ago I never thought that I'd feel this way again

Then again the excitement of knowing you

Holding you

Your soft lips

I fight from kissing you

I fight

*Closure*

Start something real with you

But I knew that when you left that we were through

And it's that feeling that had me confused

It was the knowing that I would no longer see you

Speak to you

That drew me closer to you

'Cause in hoping that we would some day

Would be the result of me wishing that your love would crumble

Your happiness I'd undo

When your happiness is all I want for you

So I'll cherish this day

Like I would cherish any other

The difference with this day

Is that it was spent with a lover

The day I loved her

# Reminder

Every morning when I wake up I hear, "thank him"

Many times I forget to

Going numb from the many things circling my thoughts

Family drama, lack of love, community turmoil

Concern for my son, kind of makes it hard to, "thank him"

So I do

Granted I may not always, but it's always on my list

My to do list

Be a better father

Be a better man

Make it as an artist

Author, musician, rapper, singer, poet

It doesn't actually matter

As long as it doesn't end with me working for the man

So my list gets wider

Adding more to each task

I hear a whisper say, "patience"

Laughing to myself as if it's that easy

I take the time to reflect

Sometimes depression sets in

That's common giving the fact of how meager I live

But then I hear again, "patience"

I shake my head

Trying to make it and failing

Makes me feel less than worth it

Some days I feel worthless

Especially going to work for a company that isn't worth it

It's disheartening

So I look at my phone

A picture of my son, has me smiling

"Fight for him"

Yes, that's what waking up has been about

Striving to accomplish something I can give to my son

I watch the sun, as it sets

Practicing my set fighting for breath

In the background I hear, "Timing"

Alone with my guitar I keep my foot tapping

Resting my fingers on my phone

I tweet for support

Found out most who know me have no arches

They're flat footed

And yet again I hear, "time to thank him"

Watching the clock

Listening to MF at 4am

I thank him for another day

Hoping that when I wake at 6

I remember to do it again

# Glossary